Taking
CHARGE

Taking CHARGE

236 PROVEN PRINCIPLES OF EFFECTIVE LEADERSHIP

BYRD BAGGETT

RUTLEDGE HILL PRESS®

Nashville, Tennessee

A Thomas Nelson Company

Byrd Baggett is an entrepreneur and a nationally acclaimed author and motivational speaker. He has written ten best-selling books, which have been published in eight languages.

For additional information, contact Baggett Consulting, P.O. Box 1190, Fairhope, AL 36533-1190. Voice: (334) 929-1237; Fax: (334) 929-1239; E-mail: byrdbaggett@bigplanet.com; Website: www.byrdbaggett.com

Copyright © 1995 by Byrd Baggett

Published by Rutledge Hill Press, a Thomas Nelson Company, P.O. Box 141000, Nashville, Tennessee 37214.

Typography by E. T. Lowe, Nashville, Tennessee.
Design by Bruce Gore, Gore Studio.

Library of Congress Cataloging-in-Publication Data

Baggett, Byrd.
    Taking charge : 236 proven principles of effective leadership / Byrd Baggett.
        p.   cm.
    ISBN 1-55853-458-X
    1. Leadership. I. Title.
HD57.7.B34   1995
658.4'092—dc20   95-39699
                                                              CIP

Printed in Colombia
2 3 4 5 6 7 8 — 06 05 04 03 02 01

*To all our loyal and dedicated
Steak-Out employees:
Without you, we could not be living the
American dream!*

*Thanks also to my wife, Jeanne, for her
unceasing support and encouragement. She
is my best friend, business partner, and the
true leader of our company.*

Introduction

AFTER TWO DECADES in sales, I never dreamed that one day I would find myself unemployed. All my life I had worked for others, achieving the kind of success that convinced me this would be my way of life until I retired. I was shocked.

Suddenly, my wife, Jeanne, and I were confronted with having to support our family with no regular income. After much soul-searching, we finally decided that the best route for us was to start our own business. Jeanne and I plunged right into some research. After evaluating several opportunities, we decided to open a food-delivery company. It was a good choice. We have been fortunate in that our business has enjoyed considerable success as one of the top franchise units in our organization.

We have learned many things as our operation has grown. At the top of the list is the realization that we didn't become true leaders the day we started our business. Our understanding of effective leadership had actually begun many years earlier while we were taking responsibility for the companies at which we worked. Unwittingly, we had received an extensive education in management and in leadership. Along the way, we developed attitudes, value systems, business strategies, and some surprisingly innovative perspectives on leadership that prepared us for flying solo! All those years of watching and interacting with successful people had rubbed off, instilling within us a sense of what it takes to lead others and thus form a successful, customer-oriented leadership style.

The leadership style that still makes the most sense to us is servant leadership as developed by Robert K. Greenleaf, a forty-year veteran of management development and education at AT&T, founder of the Center for Applied Ethics (renamed the Robert K. Greenleaf Center in 1985), and author of the 1970 essay "The Servant as Leader." Larry Spears, executive director of the Greenleaf Center, identified ten characteristics of the servant-leader: listening, empathy, healing, awareness, persuasion, conceptualization, foresight, stewardship, commitment to the growth of people, and community building. But this book is not an explanation of servant leadership. Rather it is the result of acquired knowledge and subsequent experience by one who attempts to follow the teachings of the greatest servant-leader, Jesus Christ.

Taking Charge is the third book in a trilogy featuring business principles presented in the form of easy-to-read-and-remember suggestions. Like its two predecessors, *The Book of Excellence* and *Satisfaction Guaranteed*, *Taking Charge* is a compendium of decades of hands-on experience, featuring tidbits of success gathered along the way. Whereas those two earlier books dealt mainly with the pursuit, care, and servicing of customers and clients, *Taking Charge* takes you to the next level of business, offering time-tested guidelines for successful leadership.

I hope these insights will encourage and enlighten you on your way to excellence, whether you are a veteran executive looking for a new idea or two, or just starting out in your business career. Consider *Taking Charge* your leadership compass, always available to help get you back on track when you find yourself veering off in the wrong direction. These proven ideas will enhance your success whether you are a CEO or a young employee looking for excellence. Good luck in your pursuit of the American Dream!

—Byrd Baggett

First and foremost, a good
leader serves others.

Your ability to serve others
starts with mastering yourself.

Answer the door when
opportunity knocks.

Make finding a solution a
higher priority than
placing blame.

Provide the sky in which others can soar.

Leaders visualize results.

Surround yourself with talent better than your own and carefully nurture it.

True leaders focus on delegating instead of doing.

Goals are dreams
with deadlines.

Leaders solve today's
problems while looking to
tomorrow's opportunities.

Keep asking questions and listen closely to the answers.

Leaders see more in others than others see in themselves.

Praise in public.
Criticize in private.

Milquetoast leadership is
not the breakfast
of champions.

True leaders put the
common good ahead of
personal gain.

&

Leaders perform for results,
not recognition.

Failure to take a risk is much worse than taking a risk that leads to failure.

A leader's worst decision is the one that is never made.

Putting ethics into practice
involves courage more
than conviction.

Good leaders are both
born *and* made.

If you grasp for power,
it will slip away.

&

Leaders learn from the past,
focus on the present, and
prepare for the future.

Give employees some breathing room. Be "invisible" one day every other week.

℃

Leaders understand the power of synergy.

An in-person visit beats a
written memo every time.

A leader's state of mind
affects every person
in the organization.

A genuine show of vulnerability often brings great rewards.

Most solutions are simple.

Make important decisions
only when you are alert
and relaxed.

A leader is continually
developing character
and competence.

Be teachable. You don't know everything.

Leaders realize that knowledge and skill are of no value without the fuel of motivation.

Coercion kills the
corporate spirit.

The effective leader instills
commitment to, not mere
compliance with, the
shared vision.

A good leader is a person of both action and intellect.

*

Listen to feedback carefully.

A willingness to encourage
change keeps you
moving forward.

℃

Lead people,
not organizations.

Reserve fifteen minutes
a day for yourself for
uninterrupted quiet time.

Trust your judgment and be
willing to act on it.

Be willing to sacrifice.

"I care about you."
Say it, mean it,
and live it.

Manage yourself;
lead others.

Take initiative and
encourage others to do
the same.

Expect people to perform
only as well as the example
you set.

The path to success is
often illogical.

A timid employee is the result of a tyrant.

Leaders can take charge without always being in control.

Beware of shortcuts while looking for ways to minimize the effort needed for desired results.

Be accessible and accountable.

Trust your gut feeling;
it's usually right.

A leader has a sense of
humility.

leader has a sense of
history.

leader has a sense of
humor.

True sincerity is a rare but valuable leadership trait.

❦

Each week select two items from your to-do list and delegate them to a capable employee.

Kindness is not weakness.

&

Leaders look at life through
the windshield, not the
rear-view mirror.

Continue to work on your communication skills—both written and verbal.

℃

Leaders look for great ideas, not just consensus.

Be flexible.

True leadership involves not only the exercise of authority but also full acceptance of responsibility.

Visit each associate's work
area at least once a month.

Uncertainties are a part of
life. Accept them.

A soft word
turns away anger.

Ask your associates, "What
would you do?" Expect
powerful results.

Bold leaders choose the
playing field over
the sidelines.

Set priorities
and live by them.

Encourage decision-making
at all levels.

Integrity and humility are the
leader's two best friends.

Good leadership is much deeper than personal appearance or rhetoric.

Always try to empower others to do their best.

Share your knowledge
with associates.

In solving a problem, first
look for flaws in the
organizational structure rather
than in the people.

Give others a second, third, and fourth chance.

Follow the channels of authority. And remember that it works both ways.

Small acts of recognition are
very important.

A leader willing to share
the power enhances consensus
decision-making.

Avoid the quick fix.

Before you critique another's behavior, list five positive things about that person.

Look for ways to make other people's jobs more challenging *and* fulfilling.

Anticipate chaos and be prepared to work through it.

Decisions should be based
on the core values
of an organization.

Leaders have an innate
ability to bring out the
best in others.

Leaders realize that a house divided will fall.

&

Organizations that encourage everyone's participation have an inside track to success.

Employees want to be heard
and understood.

Leaders provide others with
hope for the future.

Devote your time and energy to positive people and positive thoughts.

Learn from failure. Don't be crippled by it.

Your rules apply to you, too.

Have a genuine concern for those you lead.

Exert your will through
persuasion, not intimidation.

❦

Greet everyone with a
smile and salutation
each morning.

The leader who chooses to chase mice eventually gets trampled by the elephants.

You are in partnership with the associates you serve.

Real leaders are mentors.

&

Respect another's dignity.
Never blame or
be judgmental.

Be firm but fair.

Listen with your heart as
well as your head.

A leader puts empathy
ahead of authority.

Use your drive time to and
from work to listen to
motivational tapes.

A good decision today beats the "perfect" decision next week.

The path of least resistance is not always the best choice.

A healthy organization improves the lives of its individuals.

No decision should be made in isolation.

Give others the benefit
of the doubt.

Good leaders know how
to help others achieve
their full potential.

A strong leader places
effectiveness ahead
of efficiency.

Leadership is about
stewardship, not ownership.

Be willing to laugh
at yourself.

Send everyone home two
hours early one day
next week.

Change three bad habits
a year—you will get
phenomenal results!

Seek wise counsel.

The harder a leader pushes, the more he or she pulls the organization down.

Leaders focus on guiding, not ruling.

Time and energy spent
worrying are wasted.

Be real.
Others know when you're
just going through the
motions of good leadership.

Giving associates a chance to demonstrate their skills will develop their confidence.

Leaders willingly spend extra time with those who want to improve.

Continue to find new ways
to support those
around you.

Do not lower
your standards to
accommodate others.

Be willing to create openings
for exceptional people, even
when a position isn't
currently available.

Exercise regularly.

Eat properly.

Examine your health
consistently.

Develop meaningful
relationships at every level.

Be courteous.

We are what we watch,
listen to, and read.

If necessary, agree
to disagree.

Never use others
for self-gain.

A true leader trains
others to lead.

Avoid the temptation to blame outside circumstances for your problems.

Keep a journal and write in it daily.

An effective organization
functions as a community,
not as a family.

True loyalty is only that
which is volunteered.

A leader understands and supports the highest priorities of others.

Challenges and tests go with the territory.

Don't feel you have to
do it all yourself.

Watch out for the
"squeaky wheel."

Leaders are not
control freaks.

Envision goals as the
targets and habits
as the arrows.

Never carry a grudge.

The trick to getting angry is not losing your temper.

Be willing to forgive
yourself, too.

Give others credit
for your success.

Failure sends a leader in a new direction toward his or her next success.

Offer incentives that encourage others to take risks.

Learn from the past, but don't be paralyzed by it.

Realize that we live in the real world, not an ideal one.

A reprimand should build up, not tear down.

Lead a balanced life and encourage the same in those you lead.

Leaders are willing
to swim upstream.

Accept blame as well
as fame.

Look for ways to relieve stress in those around you.

Think of work as an adventure and instill a sense of exploration in others.

Leaders understand the fragility and importance of others' self-esteem.

Instill confidence, not confusion, in those you lead.

Emulate the leadership
habits of Vince Lombardi:
discipline, hard work, and
commitment.

Leaders accept losing
with dignity.

Remember that "silent" and "listen" contain the same letters.

An open-door policy should be exactly that.

Walk a mile in another
person's shoes before
passing judgment.

A leader tackles problems
by helping associates choose
the solution.

Put out a suggestion box,
read the contents once a
week, and act on them.

A shared philosophy and
shared experiences sharpen
your team's cohesion.

Help people produce results
they can be proud
of personally.

Always keep in mind that
what others tell you is only
the tip of the iceberg.

Illustrate your spoken vision with metaphors.

Be cognizant of the unwritten rules that govern the organization.

True rapport within an organization cannot be developed without a commitment to truth.

A leader must earn respect, not demand it.

Just because you find a problem doesn't mean the system is broken.

Develop a spirit of community, one individual at a time.

If you feel your associates
frequently let you down,
explore those feelings with
your mentor.

Share your joy with others.

A company's shared vision
must be in harmony with the
personal visions of
its individuals.

Leaders are originals,
not duplicates.

Leaders are there when needed, not only when it is convenient for them.

Use "we" instead of "me."

Choose what is right
instead of what
is politically correct.

Consult your conscience.

The art of persuasion begins with an open mind and open ears, not an open mouth.

Leaders often take the unconventional road.

Know the difference
between a rash decision and
a prompt one.

Tell those you lead what
they *need* to hear, not what
you think they *want* to hear.

Leaders are people-serving,
not self-serving.

Use a variety of stories and
anecdotes to convey the
organization's history
and philosophy.

Roll up your sleeves and
get your hands dirty.

Inside every person are seeds
of greatness. Your task
is to cultivate them.

Accept responsibility for
those you lead.

Good leaders are like baseball
umpires: They go practically
unnoticed when doing
their job right.

An apology is the sign
of a secure leader.

Managers rely on manuals.
Leaders rely on instinct.

Always focus on
the big picture.

Accept people for who and
what they are, regardless of
how different they are
from you.

Be aware of an associate's obstacles to success and work together to find the answers.

Stand tall through it all.

Leaders never put others on
the firing line until
they are ready.

Allow ample time for
reflection and dreaming.

A leader always appears
calm and cool,
never confused.

Be quick to throw a lifeline
to someone about to be
swept under.

A good leader aspires to be a role model rather than a hero.

A real leader wears Velcro instead of Teflon where acceptance of responsibility is concerned.

The abuse of power and
people will eventually
result in failure.

A good plan has a clearly
defined objective clearly
communicated to everyone.

A leader living on the edge might unwittingly push others off the cliff.

Leaders practice what they preach.

Mistakes are a necessary
part of the success process.

Potential results when
expressed should fascinate and
energize your team.

A leader balances logic and emotion.

You must be yourself to be at peace.

Every action should have a
clear purpose.

Find your passion and make
it work toward the
common good.

Encourage participation.

Practice Stephen Covey's three character traits of greatness: integrity, maturity, and abundance mentality.

TEAM means "Together Everyone Achieves More."

Employees who are given positive feedback work harder and accomplish more.

Leaders look at others as equals, not as subordinates.

Be consistently authentic and genuine. If you lose people's trust, it's almost impossible to regain it.

A prudent leader
understands the risk/reward
relationship.

Don't let your ego
get in the way.

The best concept cannot withstand poor leadership.

Leaders respect those they serve.

Be willing and prepared
to promote.

Keep in touch with the
work being done.

Treat all that you do as
work in progress.

Share both the work
and the wealth.

Leaders look for
the good in others.

Build camaraderie.

An organization's value is measured as much by the meaning it has for its employees as it is by net profits.

Learn the power of silence.

Encourage change and
new ideas. Don't be
intimidated
by them.

Enthusiasm is a way of life,
not an emotion.

Small changes often
produce big results.

A group of people
committed to a shared
vision can accomplish
the impossible.